ANIMAL ARTS AND CRAFTS

OCEAN
ANIMAL CRAFTS

Annalees Lim

Gareth Stevens
PUBLISHING

CONTENTS

SAFETY PRECAUTIONS

We recommend adult supervision at all times while doing the activities in this book. Always be aware that craft materials may contain allergens, so check the packaging for allergens if there is a risk of an allergic reaction. Anyone with a known allergy must avoid these.

- Wear an apron and cover surfaces.
- Tie back long hair.
- Ask an adult for help with cutting.
- Check materials for allergens.

BEFORE YOU START

Which ocean animals do you know about? Would you like to make some of your own and find out lots of fun facts about them along the way?

Follow the easy step-by-step instructions to create your own ocean animal collection. When you have finished making an animal, you can also think about where it might live, whether on the seabed or by the shore.

A lot of the projects use paint and glue. When you use either of them, always cover surfaces with layers of old newspaper. Whenever you can, leave the project to dry before moving on to the next step. This avoids things getting stuck to each other or paint smudging.

Some of the equipment or materials needed to make these arts and crafts can be dangerous if they are not handled correctly. Please follow the instructions carefully and ask an adult to help you. Now get ready to make your ocean life arts and crafts and discover lots of fascinating facts as well.

PAPIER-MÂCHÉ TURTLE

Sea turtles are great swimmers. They spend most of their lives underwater, returning to the surface to breathe. A turtle can swim nonstop for weeks at a time!

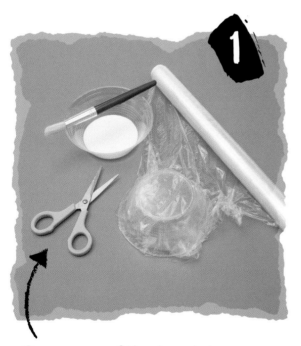

1

Cover one of the bowls in cling wrap. Use the other bowl to mix some water with the same amount of glue.

2

Cut squares of brown and green tissue paper. Stick three layers of green squares onto the bowl. Decorate with brown squares and leave to dry.

Scrunch up tissue paper. Dip it into green paint to print a pattern on the green card stock.

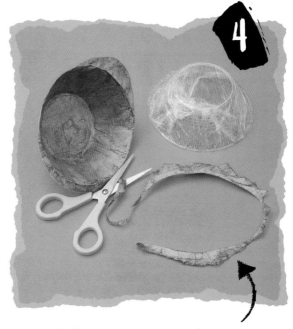

Carefully remove the tissue paper shell from the bowl. Ask an adult to help you trim the edges.

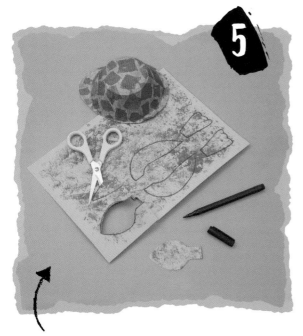

Cut out a head, tail, and four flippers from the card stock and stick them on with tape.

DID YOU KNOW?

Sea turtles can weigh over 1,100 pounds (500 kg). That's about as much as a small car!

SEA TURTLE FACTS!

Sea turtles are reptiles.

Sea turtles don't have any teeth!

Female sea turtles return to the beach where they hatched to lay their eggs.

JELLYFISH FACTS!

Jellyfish are ancient. They've lived in the oceans for at least 500 million years.

These moon jellyfish have to watch out for leatherback sea turtles. They eat jellyfish.

PLASTIC BAG JELLYFISH

Jellyfish come in many different shapes and sizes. Some can be as big as a human! You can make yours as big or as small as you like.

YOU WILL NEED:

- Large plastic sandwich bags
- White pipe cleaners
- White and pale pink curling ribbon
- Tape
- Scissors
- Ruler
- An adult to help you

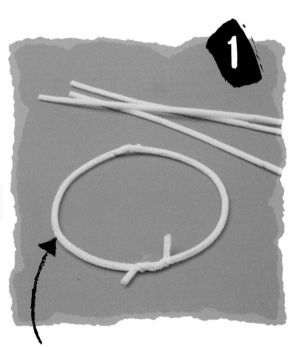

Twist the ends of two pipe cleaners together and bend them to form a circle.

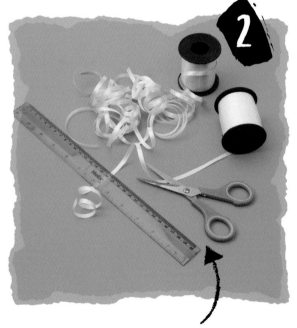

Ask an adult to help you cut long lengths of ribbon. Curl the ends by firmly running them over the edge of a ruler.

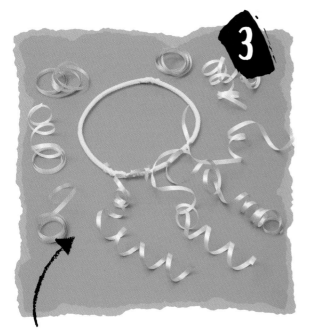

Tie the curled ribbon strands to the pipe cleaner ring.

Tie a knot into each sealed corner of the plastic bag. Turn the bag inside out and stick its open side to the ring.

Cut long strips of plastic from the other bags. Stick one end of each strip to the knots inside your jellyfish. Add a loop of plastic to the top to hang it up.

DID YOU KNOW?

Most jellyfish are see-through, like this plastic bag jellyfish!

TISSUE PAPER CORAL REEF

Coral reefs are found in warm, shallow seas. They are home to thousands of different kinds of ocean animals.

1

Cut a curved shape out of yellow card stock. Cover the cup in a layer of double-sided tape. Remove the tape's backing and wind yarn around the cup until it is covered.

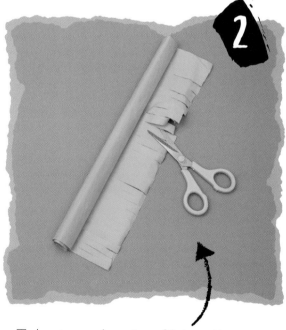

2

Take two sheets of blue tissue paper and roll them into a tube. Cut fringe into the open edge. It will be an anemone.

Flatten the tube and roll it up. Secure it with double-sided tape. Make more anemones.

Roll up some tissue paper to make branching corals. Stand some in the paper cup. Tape others together.

Glue all the anemones and corals onto the yellow card stock. Fill the gaps by scrunching up tissue paper into balls and sticking them on too.

DID YOU KNOW?

The world's biggest coral reef is Australia's Great Barrier Reef. It is 8,000 years old!

CORAL REEF FACTS!

A coral reef is made up of thousands of tiny animals called polyps. Many get their energy from even tinier plants that live inside their bodies.

Coral reefs provide homes and hiding places for animals including anemones, fish, octopuses, seahorses, and sea stars.

The stinging tentacles
of anemones keep
clown fish safe
from predators.

Seahorses hold
onto plants and
coral reefs to
keep from being
washed away.

CLOWN FISH HOME

Clown fish have a very special home: they live in the tentacles of sea anemones. You can make your very own clown fish in its home!

YOU WILL NEED:

- Four sheets of Bubble Wrap, about 8 x 12 inches each (20 x 30 cm)
- Four sheets of tissue paper (same size as above)
- Glue stick and glue
- Foam craft egg
- Wooden skewer
- Orange paint
- Paintbrush
- Tape
- Black marker
- Yellow and orange card stock
- Googly eyes
- Scissors
- An adult to help you

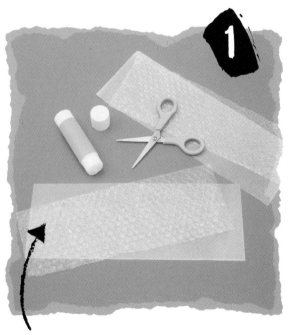

Cut the Bubble Wrap and tissue paper in half, lengthwise. Glue them together along one long edge. Repeat with different sheets of tissue paper.

Make scissor cuts and roll up each paper to form anemones with wavy tentacles. Use tape to stop them from unrolling. Stick all the tubes onto the yellow card stock.

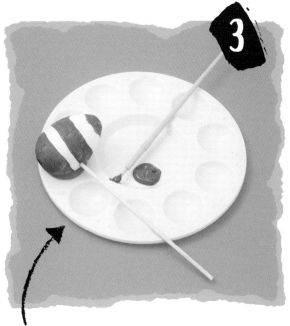

Ask an adult to help you press the foam egg onto the skewer. Paint on thick orange stripes. Leave to dry.

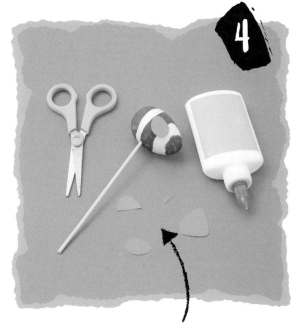

Cut out fins and a tail from the orange card stock. Stick them onto the body of your clown fish.

Use the marker to add details to your fish. Glue on googly eyes. Place the clown fish wooden skewer inside an anemone.

PAPER PLATE SEAHORSES

YOU WILL NEED:

- Paper plate
- Colorful tissue paper
- Glue stick
- Black felt-tip pen
- Scissors
- Googly eyes
- An adult to help you

Seahorses often swim in pairs, linked together by their tails. You can make two seahorses from one paper plate. Then you can link yours too!

1

2

Ask an adult to help you with the cutting in this project. Draw a seahorse shape along the edge of your paper plate. Cut it out with scissors.

Trace around this shape on the other side of the plate. Cut this seahorse out too. Cover your seahorses in glue using the glue stick.

Stick strips of colorful tissue paper onto your seahorses. Fold the ends around the edge of the seahorses. Glue them in place.

Cut a fin for each seahorse out of the paper plate. Cover the fins in tissue paper and glue them on.

Use the felt-tip pen to add details. Glue a googly eye on each seahorse.

DID YOU KNOW?

Seahorses are fish. Some kinds of seahorses stay with the same mate for life.

BALLOON WHALE

Blue whales are the largest animals that have ever lived on Earth. They can grow to 100 feet (30 m) long. Their tongues can weigh as much as an elephant!

Ask an adult to help you use the compass, ruler, and scissors to cut out a circle of dark blue card stock 4 inches (10 cm) across. Push toy stuffing into the balloon and stick on the googly eye.

Cut two strips of dark blue card stock and one strip of white card stock. All should be 12 inches (30 cm) long. Cut a wavy pattern into one long edge of each strip.

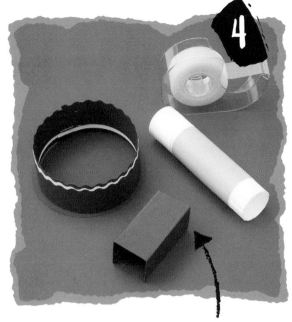

Layer the strips with the white one in the middle. Staple together. Stick the paper ring onto the blue circle with tape.

Cut out a rectangle from the dark blue card stock. Fold the rectangle to make a box and stick it down in the center of the circle.

Cut a tail out of the light blue card stock and attach it using tape. Use the pen to draw the whale's mouth. Now glue the whale onto the box.

DID YOU KNOW?

A blue whale's heart is the same size as a small car!

BLUE WHALE FACTS!

Blue whales are huge, but they eat tiny sea animals called krill. They eat up to 40 million krill a day!

Blue whales often live alone or in small groups. They call to other whales by making noises that travel through water.

Blue whales live to about 80 or 90 years old.

People hunted blue whales in the past. Slowly their numbers are increasing around the world.

Whales are mammals, so they have to swim to the surface to breathe air.

21

HERMIT CRAB

Hermit crabs live inside empty sea snail shells. They carry their shell with them wherever they go. Give your crab a home that stands out from the crowd!

YOU WILL NEED:

- Small paper plate
- Orange pom-poms (one large, two small)
- Orange pipe cleaners
- Double-sided tape
- Sequins
- Scissors
- Orange foam
- Stapler
- Glue
- Googly eyes
- An adult to help you

Stick a layer of double-sided tape along the rim of the paper plate. Take off the backing and scatter some sequins on top.

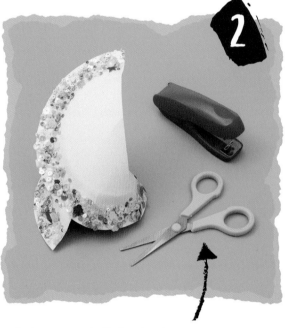

Ask an adult to help you cut into the plate, but stop short of cutting it in half. Curl the plate into a shell shape and secure it in place with a staple.

22

3

Twist four pipe cleaners together in the center and spread them out to form a star shape.

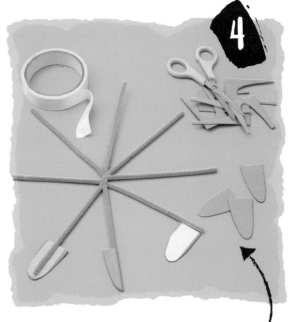

4

Cut six shapes from orange foam as shown. Use double-sided tape to stick and wrap each foam cone around a pipe cleaner.

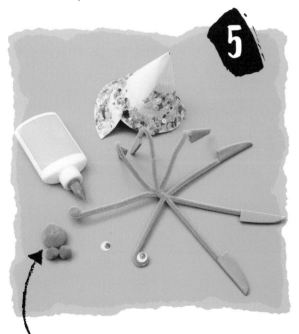

5

Curl the ends of the remaining pipe cleaners and glue on googly eyes. Tape the pipe cleaners to the inside of the shell. Glue the pom-poms behind the eye stalks.

DID YOU KNOW?

A hermit crab's shell is not just its home. It also protects the crab's body, which is very soft.

HERMIT CRAB FACTS!

As a hermit crab grows, its shell home becomes too small, so it searches for a bigger one. Then it swaps one shell home for another. It will do this many times during its life.

Hermit crabs don't act like lonely hermits at all! They usually live with other hermit crabs.

SEA STAR FACTS!

Sea stars are not fish! They are invertebrates, or have no backbone.

There are about 1,600 different kinds of sea stars. They are also sometimes called starfish.

SANDPAPER SEA STAR

Sea stars live at the bottom of seas and oceans. You can sometimes find them in rock pools too. Make these sea stars and you can keep them anywhere in your home!

YOU WILL NEED:

- Sandpaper
- Crayons
- Pencil
- Ruler
- Scissors
- An adult to help you

Use the crayons to draw small circles all over the rough sandpaper to make your sea star's spiny skin.

Turn the sandpaper over. Draw a five-point star shape onto the smooth back using the ruler and pencil.

Draw a line through each point of your star. The lines all meet in the center. Cut out your sea star.

Round off each point of the star using scissors.

Fold the sea star along each line and then pinch each point, to form the arms of your sea star.

DID YOU KNOW?

If a sea star loses one of its arms, it can grow a new one!

WOOL SWEATER SHARK

Did you know that sharks have many rows of teeth? They lose so many teeth in their lifetime that they need to grow thousands of new ones!

YOU WILL NEED:

- Old blue or gray wool sweater
- White and blue foam
- Googly eyes
- Fabric glue
- Embroidery thread
- Toy stuffing
- Scissors
- Ruler
- An adult to help you

Ask an adult to help you cut the sleeve off an old sweater. It needs to measure 12 inches (30 cm). Turn it inside out and tie the cut end together with embroidery thread.

Turn the sleeve back the right way and fill it with the toy stuffing. Fold the cuff in on itself and glue the ends together to form the mouth.

Cut out two rows of white teeth from the foam. Glue them into the mouth.

Cut out fins and a tail from the blue foam and glue them on.

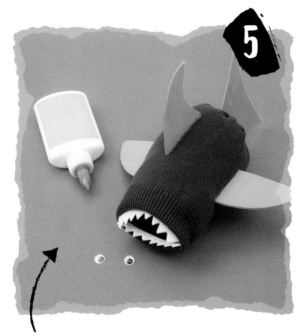

Glue on the googly eyes to finish your shark.

DID YOU KNOW? *Sharks have a great sense of smell. People sometimes call them swimming noses!*

29

PINK FOAM SHRIMP

There are many different kinds of shrimp. A lot of them live in the depths of the ocean. They swim up to the surface to feed on tiny plants and animals.

YOU WILL NEED:

- Pink foam
- Pink pipe cleaners
- Double-sided tape
- Black marker
- Scissors
- Stapler
- Ruler
- An adult to help you

Using the black marker, draw some shapes on the pink foam: a heart shape, five circles, and a tail shape.

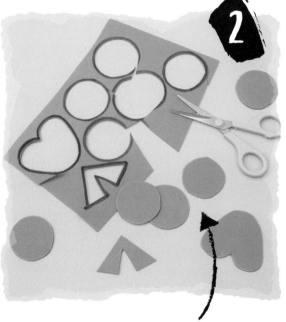

Cut out each of the shapes. Make sure you cut inside the lines to remove the black lines of the marker.

Cut a foam square, 4 x 4 inches (10 x 10 cm). Staple it to form a cylinder. Next, cut a small rectangle and cut slits into one end.

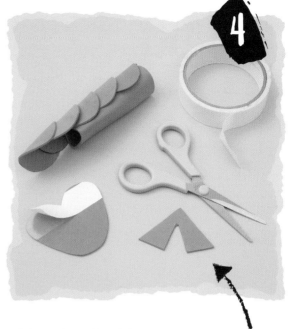

Use the double-sided tape to stick the circles onto the cylinder body. Next, stick on the heart-shaped head and the tail. Flatten the tail end of the body.

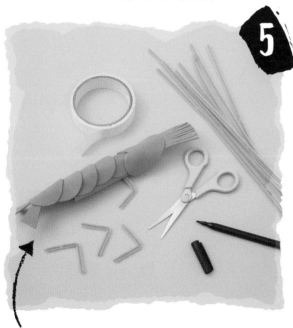

Stick the fringed foam rectangle under the head. Cut pipe cleaners to form legs and feelers. Ask an adult to help you poke them through the foam. Draw on eyes.

DID YOU KNOW?

A shrimp has five pairs of walking legs and five pairs of swimming legs.

GLOSSARY

anemone a sea animal that spends its life attached to rocks or stones

hermit someone who lives apart from others

mammal an animal with hair that gives birth to live young, and feeds its young milk

mate the partner of an animal

predator an animal that hunts and eats other animals

reptile a cold-blooded animal with scaly skin

tentacles long, thin parts of an animal's body that may be used to feel, grasp, and hold things

INDEX

Please visit our website, www.garethstevens.com. For a free color catalog of all our high-quality books, call toll free 1-800-542-2595 or fax 1-877-542-2596.

Published in 2025 by **Gareth Stevens Publishing**
2544 Clinton St.
Buffalo, NY 14224

First published in Great Britain in 2022
by Wayland

Copyright © Hodder and Stoughton, 2022

Acknowledgements:
Shutterstock: Chase Dekker 21b; Asfen Kurit 13tr; Victoria Kurtlo 25; Susana Martins 24; Shane Myers 6; Bill Roque 7; Andrew Sutton 20-21c; Veronica 12-13c; Richard Whitcombe 13br.

Every effort has been made to clear copyright. Should there be any inadvertent omission please apply to the publisher for rectification.

Cataloging-in-Publication Data
Names: Lim, Annalees.
Title: Ocean animal crafts / Annalees Lim.
Description: New York : Gareth Stevens Publishing, 2025. | Series: Animal arts and crafts | Includes glossary and index.
Identifiers: ISBN 9781538294444 (pbk.) | ISBN 9781538294451 (library bound) | ISBN 9781538294468 (ebook)
Subjects: LCSH: Handicraft--Juvenile literature. | Marine animals in art--Juvenile literature.
Classification: LCC TT160.L56 2025 | DDC 745.5--dc23

Editor, and author of the fact pages: Sarah Ridley
Design: Collaborate
Craft photography: Simon Pask, N1 Studios

Printed in the United States of America

CPSIA compliance information: Batch #CSGS25: For further information contact Gareth Stevens at 1-800-542-2595.

Find us on